THE BOY'S CHANGING VOICE

New Solutions for Today's Choral Teacher

BY TERRY J. BARHAM AND DAROLYNE L. NELSON

4MPS0000207597

Terry J. Barham, Ph.D.
Emporia State University
Emporia, Kansas

Darolyne L. Nelson
Mckerny Middle School
Tempe, Arizona

Design/Illustrations:
Ken Rehm

ACKNOWLEDGMENTS

We are indebted to many individuals for their inspiration and support. Thanks to John Cooksey for his in-depth studies of the boy's changing voice. A majority of the ideas expressed in this book concerning voice change in adolescent boys is drawn from his research. Thanks to Audrey Snyder Brown, Editor for CPP/Belwin, for giving us encouragement and the opportunity to publish this manual and to Brian Busch, Senior Choral Editor for CPP/Belwin, for his patient guidance and invaluable insights into writing and organizing the manuscript. Thanks to Wallace Long, Jr. for sharing many ideas for vocalises. Thanks to our former teachers and many colleagues, particularly Barbara Andress, Ladd Bausch, Robert Carnes, Donald Hoiness, Elisabeth Parham, Gail De Stwolinski, and Clara (Suggie) Thompson for believing in us and sharing their wisdom about people and teaching and the deeper values and beauty of music and singing. To our spouses, Terry and Susan, we say thank you for your patience and love throughout this project.

CONTENTS

INTRODUCTION

Many directors of church and school choirs feel uncomfortable when dealing with boys' voices in their ensembles. Preparing music with a mixed chorus offers sufficient challenges without the questions which arise concerning the changing voice in boys: How do I know when a boy's voice is beginning to change? How do I classify these voices? What do I do with the boy who sings everything an octave lower than written? Should boys be singing when the voice change process seems most noticeable? What exercises will promote healthy singing habits and aid in the development of free and beautiful singing? How can I choose music which will fit the boys' voices? What can I do about boys' attitudes about singing?

Before discussing these questions and possible answers, let's briefly review three approaches to the classification of male voice change which emerged in the 1950's and 1960's. Figure 1 indicates the designation of pitches and ranges used throughout this manual, giving us a common reference point when discussing the various approaches to classifying boys' voices.

Figure 1. Pitch Level Designators

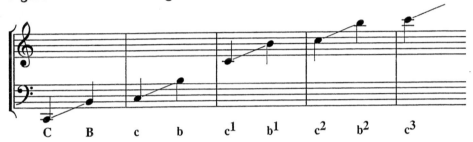

$$C \quad B \quad c \quad b \quad c^1 \quad b^1 \quad c^2 \quad b^2 \quad c^3$$

Irvin Cooper coined the term "cambiata" to describe the boy's changing voice prior to becoming a baritone. He classified all boys' voices as either boy sopranos, bb-f^2; cambiata, f-c^2; or baritones, Bb-f^1. [1]

Frederick Swanson, retired director of the Moline (Illinois) Boys' Choir, applied three different classifications: boy alto, g-f^2; tenor, d-e^1; and bass, A-g. In addition, Swanson urged greater understanding of the contra-bass adolescent voice with its low notes of D and C or lower, commonly known as the "fry" tones. [2]

Duncan McKenzie, a British music educator, evolved the alto-tenor plan of classification with its six categories for boys: soprano I, c^1-g^2; soprano II, b-e^2; alto, a-c^2; alto-tenor, g-g^1; baritone, (seventh grade), c-b; and baritone (eighth and ninth grade), B-c^1. [3]

Both McKenzie and Cooper felt that the junior high bass is rare, a fact opposed by Swanson. McKenzie and Cooper also believed that the changing voice lowers at a gradual rate. Swanson found that the rate of voice change was rapid.

For us, the dilemma ended with the emergence of John Cooksey's eclectic theory of voice change in boys developed in the 1970's. [4] His six categories, which include elements of the work of Cooper, McKenzie, and Swanson, are as follows: unchanged, a-f^2; mid-voice I, a♭-c^2; mid-voice II, f-a^1; mid-voice II A, d-f♯^{1}; new baritone, B-d♯^{1}; and settling baritone, G-d^1. [5] He, like McKenzie and Cooper, felt that the rate of change for the boy's changing voice was gradual.

Cooksey's categories provided us with much food for thought. Many of the ideas and concepts expressed in this book are based on his research. However, with extensive testing and in-class application, we reduced the six categories to four and modified them slightly to approximate more nearly what we found in our work. The names of the categories were changed to include the widely-used term, "cambiata." The four resulting categories are (1) treble, a-f^2; (2) cambiata I, g-c^2; (3) cambiata II, e♭-f^1; and (4) baritone, A-d^1. See Figure 2. As might be expected, all boys do not neatly fit within these exact ranges. However, in our experiences, most boys will.

The ideas in this book grew out of classroom experiences buttressed by broad-based research findings. The opening chapter addresses the challenge of classifying boys' voices. Succeeding chapters include practical suggestions for developing positive attitudes about vocal change, selecting and adapting music, placing boys within ensembles of various types, understanding adolescent behavior, tips for effective teaching and common problems with possible solutions. The final chapter is a list of recommended choral music for various voice combinations. Four appendices offer tested vocalises.

I

PUTTING ROUND PEGS IN ROUND HOLES

VOICE PLACEMENT

Every young man deserves to know where he "fits in." As can be found under "Testing Procedures," non-threatening ways of determining a boy's vocal category can pave the way for increased self-esteem and musical growth. You should place boys into one of these four categories: Treble, Cambiata I, Cambiata II, or Baritone (Figure 2).

Figure 2. Categories and Ranges of Boys' Changing Voices

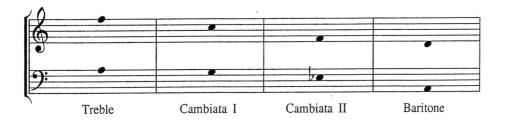

Treble   Cambiata I   Cambiata II   Baritone

"I sound great on these low parts!"

RECOGNIZING CHANGE

Cooksey indicates that the speaking voice changes before the singing voice and is a fairly reliable indicator of change. [6] The speaking voice lies near the bottom of the voice range. Changes in the singing voice proceed at various rates through the four-stage pattern beginning with Cambiata I. Change, for a majority of boys, begins at ages 12-13, is most active between 13-14, and tapers off between 15 and 18. [7] It should be noted that some boys' voices begin changing as early as the fourth and fifth grades. [8] Boys often experience loss of several pitches at the upper end of their voice ranges before adding new pitches to their lowest sung sounds.

The first signs that voice change is occurring include an increase in breathiness and physical signs of strain in the upper register. Watch for tightening neck muscles and occasional jutting jaws as boys compensate for reduced ranges and poor breath support. Boys who speak "hello" on the pitches A or A♭ below middle C (c¹) are usually Trebles (unchanged) or Cambiata I's. These young men may try to sing the tenor part, duck their heads, and growl around almost inaudibly below middle C. However, they certainly can and should sing either the soprano or the alto lines, whichever part is appropriate, so that bad habits do not develop. If you make this change, be sure to bolster the young man's esteem for himself by explaining the situation clearly and using terms to foster strong identity.

"Is that me?   Am I really a Cambiata I?"

TESTING PROCEDURES

All boys' voices should be tested every six to eight weeks, or even more frequently, during the school year. Keeping charts for all to see how each individual is progressing will foster pride and understanding of the natural growth process. The following steps are suggested for the initial testing of boys' voices:

1. If possible, test in a room apart from the girls. Boys are generally self conscious.
2. Have each boy say "hello" to you.
3. Notate the "hello" pitch on a grand staff marked off with each boy's name.

Figure 3. "Hello" Pitch and Sung Pitches

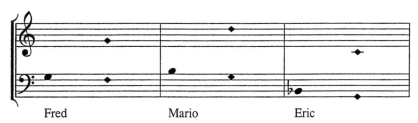

● = "Hello" pitch

◆ = sung pitch

9

4. Remember that a boy's speaking pitch lies near the bottom of his singing range.
5. Be sure that a chalkboard is used for the "hello" pitch. Boys need to see where they fit in comparison to their peers.
6. Hand all boys a copy of the chart (Figure 2) showing the four voice classifications. Tell them that, knowing where their speaking pitch lies, they can help decide their particular voice category.
7. Using the speaking pitch as 1, or "do," have each boy sing hello-o-o-o-o (do, do, re, mi, re, do), moving up by chromatic half steps until his upper range is reached. Signs of strain will tell you when to stop! Don't be afraid to let boys who sing the Baritone part change registers - go into the lighter weight falsetto sound. Be aware that some won't be able to produce falsetto yet. Have the boys, Cambiata I's, II's and Baritones, try a short hoot (like an owl) on an "oo" vowel a fifth or more above where they were able to reach using the sung "hello" pattern. They may discover that they can sing above a temporary "blank" area which sometimes occurs as the muscles in the larynx grow rapidly.
8. On the chalkboard, notate the upper singing pitch above the speaking pitch.
9. Moving down from the speaking pitch chromatically, use hello-o-o-o (mi, mi, re, do, re, mi) to find the lowest healthy sung pitch.
10. Notate the lowest pitch. Praise each boy for his persistence and for something good you heard in his singing.

Cooksey outlined the following successful group voice testing procedure.[9] Have all boys sing "America" or some other well-known song in the key of C, once with piano and then a second time without piano as you walk among the boys. All boys who sing in the lower octave are baritones. Move them together. Sing again to check for any errors you might have made. Do not be bothered by the fact that some boys will not sing in the exact key. Find a key that fits! Use only the first phrase of the song if necessary to save time.

Have the remaining boys sing "America" in the key of Eb or E. All those singing in the upper octave should be assigned to the Cambiata I or Treble part. Those singing in the lower octave (or close to it) should be assigned to Cambiata II.

TIME-SAVERS FOR TESTING VOICES

In auditioning large numbers of singers in any given day, try implementing the following helpful procedures:

1. Color code choir section cards. Using six colors of construction paper, cut shapes or stamp designs on small pieces to indicate each of the six voice groups you will hear: Soprano, Alto, Treble, Cambiata I, Cambiata II, and Baritone. As you hear each individual, hand him or her the appropriate colored card. When testing for an entire group is completed, call colors into sections. Have students write their names on a list for each section. With additional notations from you as you audition, this process can be extended to include specific seating arrangements. See "Seating Charts" in Chapter VI on page 24.

2. Students who are seated in the same room and not being tested should be given appropriate musical tasks on worksheets prepared earlier. Don't waste their time. Be sure they are productive.

3. Initial testing at the beginning of the year requires that each student's attention be focused on the actual procedure so that he or she will understand the individuality of each voice and its potential contribution to the ensemble.

VARIABLES WITH CHANGE

In Cambiata I, a reduced range may emerge. A boy may be left with a range of six or seven notes plus a "blank" spot above. This can be a prelude to change into the Cambiata II category. Teachers should not be surprised by the occasional subterranean bass - that young man with the pedal tone Bb, two octaves and a second below middle C. He may have a limited range of less than an octave. He should be encouraged to sing in his octave whichever written part will fit. If needed, write a new part for him.

Boys should know that their voices may move back into the Cambiata II range after a stopover in the Baritone category. Just because a boy may sing pitches as low as a baritone does not mean that he is a baritone forever. Change of voice, in its more subtle aspects, continues for years, even into a man's 20's. Be aware that variables are the norm.

SELF-ESTEEM AND IMAGE

All work with junior high/middle school boys (and girls) should be predicated upon the recognition of each individual's uniqueness and self-worth. No two personalities are alike. No two voices are alike in range, timbre, tone quality, or comfortable tessitura. Boys should know the whole story prior to the onset of any voice changes. They should be told that, at some point, their baby fat may drop away, their height and weight may increase rapidly, beards and pubic hair will appear, the larynx (adam's apple) will get larger, and their speaking voices may feel unstable. A fourteen-year-old boy may sing Cambiata I. A twelve-year-old may be a Baritone. It will be natural for some boys to "siren" as high as girls at one point but then experience, within several months, decreased range and power on the same exercise. Sooner or later, all boys' voices experience the process of change!

II

GOOD STROKES FOR YOUR SINGING FOLKS

CREATING A SAFE ENVIRONMENT

For these young men, a positive attitude about themselves is a natural outgrowth of understanding what is happening to their voices. Factors influencing behavior include peer pressure, the search for identity, parental support, and the need to be "normal."

Singing is personal. It requires that the boy take a chance. At stake is not only his personal esteem, but also his social identity. The choir, under the leadership of the teacher, must become a support group. You are instructing in how to "live," not just how to survive. The boy who feels confident that he will be accepted will be willing to take the chance . . .sing! Teachers should model and preach family concepts, such as caring, sharing, trusting, giving, protecting, and loving. These are strong tools for creating a nurturing environment.

BRINGING GIRLS INTO THE PICTURE

Since girls' voices also change, though not to the degree observable in boys, girls should be included in the educational process of voice placement. Such an exchange of information results in mutual support and positive attitudes in your choral program. After the initial testing at the beginning of the school year, boys and girls can be tested in the same classroom. Educating the girls in the process of male vocal development mitigates the problems which can occur in daily rehearsals - a boy's voice "breaks" and girls snicker. It is common knowledge that boys will go to great lengths to keep from "cracking" in mixed company. Girls at this age offer strong moral support for their male peers' vocal challenges. Boys will take pride in their personal growth when they are comfortable in mixed chorus rehearsals.

CHARTING VOCAL GROWTH

Keep wall charts so everyone can see how each individual is progressing. This will foster pride and understanding in the natural growth process. Such a practice contributes to male camaraderie. Two types of charting are successful: (1) On a grand staff, place the lowest and highest notes each boy sings comfortably for each grading period, and (2) Using a grand staff with four measures for each boy, write the same information for each of the grading periods as testing time is completed. Each boy's name must be clearly visible.

Figure 4. Individual Voice Ranges
September 1 - October 30

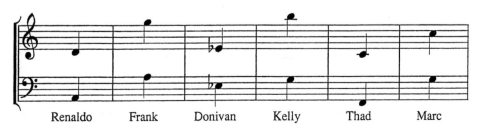

| Renaldo | Frank | Donivan | Kelly | Thad | Marc |

"Someday . . ."

VOCAL MODELS

Female teachers should bring in a mature male singer to demonstrate the falsetto voice and the natural "breaks" when a descending scale is sung from the pitch B above middle C. A male teacher should freely demonstrate the falsetto voice. Make the boys proud of the unique quality of their "high" voices, as opposed to the quality of their chest register or the loud speaking voice (See Appendix III-1). Find out who the popular male singers and singing groups are who use the falsetto voice extensively. Use their recordings as models. These examples should eliminate the misconception that high voices are feminine and low voices are masculine.

SINGING THROUGH THE CHANGE

Contrary to a number of continental European boy choir practices, boys should be encouraged to sing through the time of voice change. Observe healthy singing habits. The changes proceed at various rates through the four-stage pattern shown in Figure 2. If you are creating a supportive environment in the rehearsal, the changes will be understood, not feared. Singing, though possibly limited in range and clarity of tone, will continue for each boy.

PUTTING THE PIECES TOGETHER - THE PUZZLE OF SELECTING AND ADAPTING MUSIC

SEARCHING FOR THE PERFECT SONG

Selecting music for the boy's changing voice can be one of the most time consuming tasks you face. To discover the ideal piece is truly a rarity. A good rule of thumb is to go with the "vocal majority" and to adapt for the "vocal minority." When perusing scores, keep in mind some of the limitations of the changing voice: limited range, limited flexibility, and a minimum number of sudden register shifts. Setting up a hierarchy of evaluative criteria will save you countless hours of searching. Try the following:

1. Range and tessitura
2. Adaptability
3. Intrinsic worth and educational value
4. Lyrics/suitability of text
5. Editorial problems. Know your choir's maturity level. Avoid choosing songs which designate female voicing for the male parts. Avoid cover art work which is beneath the adolescent palette. Avoid visual layout complexity, such as bass lyrics on the alto line.

"Yes! We can do it!"

TAILORING A SONG TO MEET THE NEEDS OF THE ENSEMBLE

Several techniques can be employed when adapting music for your ensemble. Create changes which fit the majority of your boys' voices. During rehearsals, individual changes can be made, one to one, based on what you hear. Teach the boys to make the changes in their music, using a pencil. Worksheets have proven to be useful but are initially time consuming. However, the educational value of worksheets and of making changes in the music is inestimable. Work out a system of verbal and written symbols which are consistent so that the boys can become independent in making necessary adaptations. At the end of each semester, have each boy erase all of his "changes" so that the same music can be used with new singers. Experiment with the following procedures:

1. Octave Displacement. Shift a pitch up or down an octave even for only a few pitches which are out of the comfortable range.

Figure 5. Octave Displacement

2. Note Division with Octave Displacement. Repeat a pitch one octave higher or lower while shortening the rhythmic value by one-half.

Figure 6. Note Division with Octave Displacement

becomes

3. Transposition. If you have transposition skills, move the pitches up or down by one half-step from what is notated. As an aid, you can imagine placing an alto clef in front of each staff. Then read all pitches up one letter name. If the music is to be transposed down one step, imagine placing a tenor clef in front of each staff. Read all pitches down one letter name.

    Reduce the music to its harmonic skeleton using as few chords as possible (I, IV, V) and "fake" the chord progressions while reading a specific voice line. Read the arabic guitar chord symbols up or down a second. A word of caution: When rehearsing music which appears to be written in correct keys early in the morning, choirs may sharp considerably at concert time under the pressure of performance and fully warmed-up voices. Thus you or your accompanist should be prepared to transpose the music on a moment's notice.

4. Doubling Parts. Doubling occurs when two different voice parts sing the same written part in octaves. It is important to double what fits each boy's range best. Any part can be doubled. You should feel no qualms about violating the traditional choral pyramid in which the bass voice sonority is foundational and the remaining choral voices fit into a "pyramid" above that foundation. If the written part range is too wide, double at the octave and employ octave displacement.

5. Writing a New Part. Some pieces are so valuable for student growth that adding a line to fit the changing voices is warranted. Know your choir. They may make your effort on a new part worth the investment.

6. Part Skipping. Encourage students to change from one voice line to another temporarily, e.g., from Cambiata I to Alto, in order to accommodate individual range limitations. This can be done by measure or by phrase.

EENIE, MEENIE, MEINIE, MO, THIS IS WHERE HE HAS TO GO

THE Y'ALL COME CHOIR

While general chorus benefits a wide range of students because of the nature of the group and its goals, definite drawbacks occur when changing voices are involved. In most cases, the biggest problem is the overwhelming number of girls compared to boys. The result is often a frustrating situation for all involved, especially when the boys are spread among all four voice categories: Treble, Cambiata I, Cambiata II, and Baritone. Avoid the easy out of using SAB music when other categories (Cambiata I and II) are needed to promote vocal health.

The "B" part in SAB music is a great frustration for many boys because it is often too high or too low, or it's tessitura is uncomfortable. That same part is vocally unhealthy for the Trebles and Cambiatas. Singing around a♭-c¹ for them is the equivalent of asking 20-year-old tenors to sing mostly one octave below middle C or of asking sopranos to sing in the area of middle C constantly. It's very frustrating! The solution requires great care in choosing music in several parts or adapting two-part or three-part music using the suggestions found in the previous chapter.

APPROPRIATE MUSIC WITH APPROPRIATE VOICINGS

In locating challenging music that provides the best possible musical experience for your ensembles, the voicing and the number and nature of the parts must fit the needs of the choir. Consider the students' musical experience and musical growth, without vocal strain, to be the goal. Use various voicings to fit your needs, expanding and changing the number of parts as the choir's skill and vocal growth change. Consult the recommended music list in Chapter VIII on pages 27-55.

Cautionary words are in order. It is not healthy to add girls to the boys' parts in order to balance the choir. Occasional doubling of this type may be necessary, but girls should then sing literature which demands that they use the "head" voice with its lighter, flute-like weight.

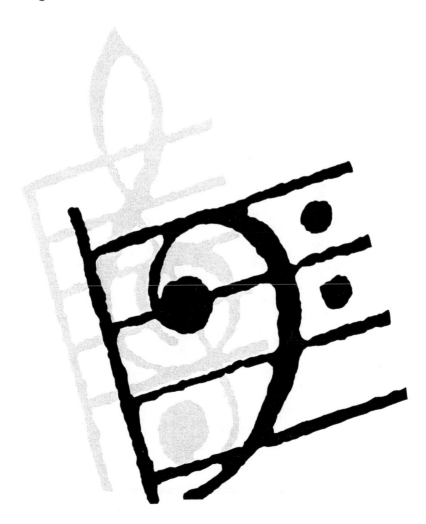

"Soprano is for girls!"

MALE IDENTITY AND VOICING TERMINOLOGY

Boys are very sensitive about where they "fit in" with the changing bodies around them - hair on legs and face, big shoulders, and developing muscles. They need to be able to look at themselves and say, "I see who I am and what is happening to me." The labeling which occurs through regular testing of voices provides these young men with a healthy identity and a source of pride.

Problems arise when the voice part labels do not jive with what the boys feel they should be singing, such as baritones being asked to sing a part labeled "soprano." Teaching your chorus about music arranging and voicing is helpful in dealing with this conflict. Basic information you could share would include choice of composer and style, range-crossing problems, and publishing/editorial requirements. Let your boys know that you have chosen or adapted the part to fit their individual need and that they are special. If needed, use the terms Part I, Part II, Part III, etc., rather than Cambiata I or II to describe the voice parts. If you know the maturity level and security reservoir of your male singers, you can save their losing face and dropping out of your program. Soprano can be a dirty word to those boys!

GROWTH THROUGH SWITCHING VOICE PARTS

Keep all choir members moving to different voice parts during the course of a semester. You should not pigeon-hole young singers by requiring that they sing the same part all year. Assigning voice parts should be based on voice range, quality of sound, and singing comfort, not on superb reading skills and outstanding leadership qualities or the lack thereof. A change of voice part provides for growth in musicianship, range, and listening skills. It also widens the students' perspectives of themselves with relation to the entire choir.

Learning to sing harmony is advantageous for Trebles, aiding their success when the voice change begins. With all singers moving from part to part between different works, the activity becomes the norm and thus an emotional benefit to the boy whose voice is changing.

V

LIFE WITH CHAMELEONS

BEHAVIORAL TRAITS

A lifetime could be spent observing and studying the characteristics of adolescents. However, one trait, the "I Love You/I Hate You" syndrome, seems to stand by itself. At one moment, you are the best teacher in the school. At another, you are the bad guy to end all bad guys. The wise teacher takes it in stride and allows the students to sort out their feelings. Emotions consistently appear to run in extremes. "I don't know" is the usual answer for any questioned behavior.

HONESTY IN APPROACH - LETTING THE KIDS "IN"

Honesty and openness are among the best tools you possess for working with adolescents. Your students watch you and all adults very carefully. They see through any facade quickly. They respond well to honest, tactful comments. If you make a mistake, don't be afraid to admit it. "My fault. Let's do it again," is common in an honest classroom.

Your love for music and your students should be general knowledge with everyone. Instead of putting on the "teacher face," be candid even while understanding the fragile nature of adolescent egos. You will win your students' respect with consistency of approach.

The "I Love You/I Hate You" syndrome, though expressed toward others, is a sign of inner turmoil and is often acted out in class. When boys become frustrated with what is happening to them vocally, they are apt to talk out of turn, punch their neighbors, or deliberately drop their music. Teacher/student confrontations can be avoided by directing the boys' attention away from the misdemeanor and by offering sincere, positive musical strokes. Sensitive teachers turn critical emotional responses into educational springboards.

TAPPING THEIR ENERGY

The boundless exuberance and energy of junior high students is renown. Your challenge is to harness and direct that energy into channels of learning. Teacher modeling of focused effort, carefully organized rehearsal plans, and enthusiasm are key elements. As successful moments are achieved and one-minute "praisings" offered, your students will zero in on musical tasks and ask for more.

Challenges excite these emerging young men and women. If they are not challenged, they tune out, die out, and get out -of music! Music is a powerful motivator. It feeds the human spirit. Using the building blocks of music to tap the emotional sensitivity of the adolescent can make working with changing voices a deeply rewarding experience, both for you and your students.

VI

TIPS FOR TRAINING THE TIGERS

STRUCTURING AND SURPRISING

Adolescents function with certainty in a classroom that has a reliable routine. Once the structure is taught to the students, valuable learning time is increased because less explaining and fewer directions are required. Placing responsibility for learning and behavior on the student by means of a consistently implemented program directs the student to form habits that also provide for increased instructional time.

On the other hand, changing routines in the class can provide stimulation and increased interest. Some changes can be as simple as moving the third row of the choir to the front row or changing sight reading exercises to a different place in the routine. Your administrative announcements should not be made at the same place in your rehearsal all of the time. Listening to recordings of fine junior high school choruses (from ACDA conventions, for instance) should spice up the routine five or six times each semester. Moving one section around the piano when zeroing in on a particularly difficult passage adds visual and aural variety to your rehearsal. Use the chalkboard to draw abstract pictures of concepts which you are teaching. In this visual age of ardent, young TV viewers, consider using less talk and more pictorial representations of your ideas.

"When is this class over?"

PROVIDING FOR CHANGING BODIES

Adolescents are prisoners of their bodies! Long periods of sitting or standing usually result in mental shut down and teacher frustration. Begin each class with body warm-ups to increase oxygen supply to the brain, relieve stress, and provide for increased accuracy in those songs which employ choreography.

Frequent changes of posture during rehearsal improve attention spans. Try breaking up an intense rehearsal by having students (1) turn to the right or left to massage shoulders and necks of students next to them, (2) stretch, bend, and pull knees to the chest while sitting on the floor, or (3) do a dozen jumping jacks in the middle of a rehearsal. While students will certainly chatter and break concentration, the positive result of physical activity will increase desired learnings.

ESTEEM-BUILDING TECHNIQUES

Positive reinforcement is a powerful and basic teaching strategy crucial for adolescents due to the psychological changes manifested during puberty. Your choir class can become a haven in which a student can feel good about himself. The following suggestions have proven successful in generating positive self-esteem:

1. Use bulletin boards to display student names at the beginning of the year. The headline might read: Central Choir-Together In Harmony!

2. Use charts which log accomplishments toward a specific goal for individual students and for the choir.

3. Design paper money, Music "Moola," that can be redeemed for various rewards, such as sheet music, cassette recordings, rock magazines or going to the lunch room for a meal with the teacher. If funds are limited, use "Moola" for drawings.

4. Invite boys from neighboring schools and male teachers from your faculty to perform at a concert once a year.

5. Use index cards to develop Teacher Praise And Prompt Cards which list adjectives for praising your singers. Keep them handy - on the piano or music stand - and use at least one card each day. Such a practice eliminates the habit of repeating one stock word or phrase such as "good, good," or "excellent, excellent!"

6. Challenge the baritones to use falsetto, the flute-like quality which develops during the Cambiata II stage (See Appendix III). Have them sing the soprano line when that part is poorly sung. Boys generally love showing up girls.

7. Be sensitive to boys' needs concerning concert apparel. Create a special look for which they will be proud.

8. Break down unhealthy music stereotypes at every opportunity. Call your boys "guys" in order to preserve male dignity and encourage male bonding. Get rid of the "wimp" image. Talk about it. Then put the term in its place - out of the vocabulary. Work at making choir classes as male oriented as they are female.

VOCALISES

Vocalises have inadvertently served non-musical purposes such as signifying to latecomers that class has started, making students get their music and sit down, and taking roll.[10] However, they are possibly the most vital part of your rehearsal. Vocalises are not a ritual which must be endured but rather a highly important activity in teaching boys how to sing properly and how to audiate sounds. Audiation is a type of inner hearing, specifically the ability to hear a tone, a chord, or a melody in one's head without that tone or chord being played or sung externally. [11] Young singers need your help in learning to audiate good tone quality, in-tune pitches, and tonal and rhythm patterns. Vocalises can be your vehicle for such training.

Specific objectives for each exercise should be written on the chalkboard and verbally directed to the class so that mindless repetition of a few exercises does not engender casual attitudes about singing. Use your music scores to derive vocalises which solve problems. Try changing your vocalises from one week to the next to challenge the students. Recommended vocalises can be found in Appendices I-IV. To meet individual needs, feel free to alter and expand the recommended vocalises. It is important **that all melodic vocalises be transposed to levels which help students rather than hinder them.**

Vocalises can be grouped into four major categories (Figure 7). Discuss these categories with your students. Have them make up vocalises which both you and they lead. If used with wisdom and patience, good vocalises will promote musical growth and healthy singing habits.

Figure 7. Vocalise Categories

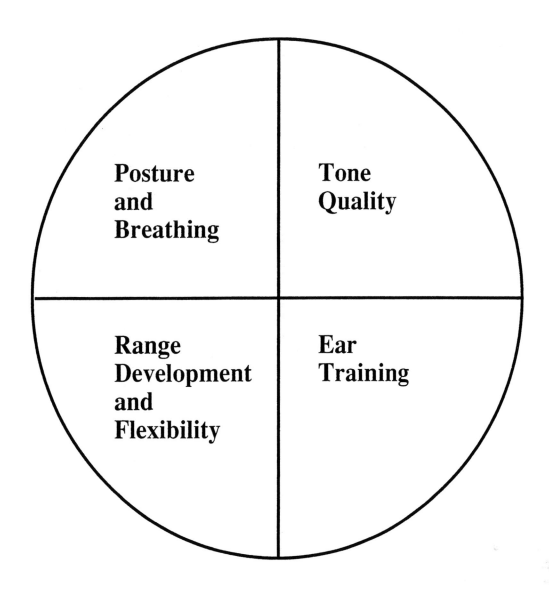

Posture and Breathing: physical awakening; hissing; belt-level (diaphragmatic) breathing while saying ABC's continuously; the surprise breath; the long, slow breath; expanded rib cage with upright alert posture (See Appendix I)

Tone Quality: basic vowels and the vowel wheel; head voice quality; chest voice quality and mixed voice quality; vowel unification; tall vowels with inner space; tonal focus (See Appendix II)

Range Development and Flexibility: baby sighs; pigeon cooing in falsetto voice; wide-range sirens across registers; consonant tongue twisters; mixing of descending and ascending melodic exercises (See Appendix III)

Ear Training: Tonal and rhythm syllable sing-back (from Edwin Gordon's Learning Sequence Activities) [12]; chord balancing; gradation of dynamics (See Appendix IV)

GORDON TONAL AND RHYTHM SYLLABLES

For five to ten minutes every other day throughout the school year, consider using the tonal and rhythm patterns developed by Edwin Gordon in his extensively tested Learning Sequence Activities.[13] These specific, sequentially organized patterns are aptitude based so that each student will experience success, which we know is a prime motivator in learning. Use tonal patterns one week and rhythm patterns the next week.

Gordon's Music Learning Theory is based on the premise that children learn music the same way they learn language. [14] See Appendix IV for specific applications. Research in language development has now established that from birth to eighteen months, children function in a babble stage in which they hear a kaleidoscopic array of individual sounds or phonemes from their environment. From approximately eighteen months to five years, children emerge from the babble stage and put phonemes together into words, phrases, and sentences. About the age of five, these children go to "school" and see the written symbols which they have heard and spoken from their environment. Only then do they begin to interpret the symbols, to read them, and finally, to write the symbols as words. Listening and speaking precede reading and writing. [15]

The same principle, sound before symbol, is at the core of Gordon's Music Learning Theory. This principle is not new. Lowell Mason employed it in the late nineteenth century when he established the first public school music education programs in the United States.

Also important in Music Learning Theory is the use of music aptitude testing which establishes the music potential of each student, thus paving the way for the success of each individual, no matter whether he or she is of low, average, or high music aptitude. An important new aptitude test appropriate for junior high/middle school students is the Advanced Measures of Music Audiation (AMMA) by Edwin Gordon. [16] The results of aptitude testing provide a basis for teaching to individual differences even in a choral ensemble. Perhaps more important, an instrumental or vocal music teacher can provide administrators and school boards with nationally standardized test results of students' achievement in music classes. In this day and age, charts and graphs showing student growth in music speak effectively to the general public.

COMMON SENSE

It goes without saying that the training of the changing voice should begin with comfortable singing ranges and tessituras. Forcing high notes, such as happens with many baritones, should be avoided. Don't ask your singers to sustain notes in their upper ranges at high dynamic levels when the singers have little understanding of proper breathing and support of tone and open, "tall" vowels (See Appendices I-III). Attention to excellent posture, belt-level diaphragmatic breathing, open mouth and active lips will give impetus to normal, free development of the singing voice. The teacher's positive attitude, humor and encouragement during vocalises are of inestimable value in nurturing the self-esteem of young singers.

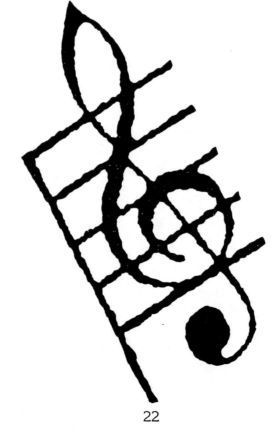

"before"

"after!"

SEATING CHARTS

Seating plans should be varied according to the needs of the music and the need of the students to become musically independent. In addition, the personal dynamics of the ensemble may require placement of individuals for acoustical reasons, such as the strident voice which masks out the singer with the flute-like quality.

Organize the boys so that they stand in close proximity to one another. The result is more assured singing. Place the boy Treble next to the baritone section rather than at the end of a girls' row. Avoid placing a single boy in a female section. Treble and Cambiata I singers can be made to feel uncomfortable by placing them by height within a girls' section. Avoid placing different voice parts behind the boys when the latter are weak singers. Group them in the center from the back row to the front.

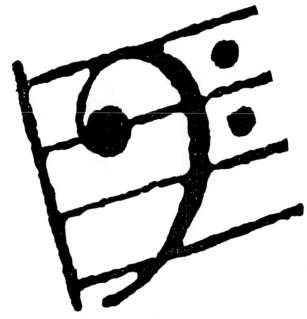

These symbols are used in the following charts:

G	Girl
T	Treble (boy)
CI	Cambiata I
CII	Cambiata II
B	Baritone
S	Soprano
A	Alto

A. Two-Part With Octave Doubling*

G	G	G	G	G		G	G	G	G	G
CII	CII	T	T	T	CI	CI	B	B	B	
	G	G	T	T	CI	CI	G	G		

* Placing girls behind boys helps boys stay on pitch.
* Adding girls to the front row changes the overall quality of the choral sound.

B. SSA/Three-Part*

Soprano I				Soprano II				Alto			
G	G	G	G	G	G	G	G	G	G	G	G
CII	CII	T	T		T	T	T	CI	CI	B	B
G	G	G	G	G	G	G	G	G	G	G	G

* This chart is a natural extension of an SA/Two-Part arrangement. Placing all boys in the second row offers visual/physical identity of boys as one-third of choir and aids in their holding harmony parts.

C. Three-Part Mixed With Unequal Balance*

G	G	G	G		B	B		G	G	G	G
	G	G		T	B	B	B	T	G	G	
	G	G		T	B	B	T	G	G		

* Place strongest boys in back. Place weakest boys in center row. Since the sound radiates in all directions, they receive help from all sides.
*Place girls with lightest weight voices next to boys.

D. SATB*

S	S	S							A	A	A
S	T	T	B	B	CII	CII	CI	CI	A	A	
S	S	S	B	B	CII	CII	A	A	A		

*Put Cambiata and Baritone sections on front of risers and leave area behind them open. Filling in with different voicings may cause pitch problems.
* Placing males in the center has a positive emotional impact and surrounds them with sound. The entire choir benefits.

24

RECRUITING

Quality and excitement about making music attract boys. Having an outstanding select ensemble is a primary recruiting tool. Arrange for concerts at feeder schools to bring attention to your choral program. Principals and counselors are more willing to assist you in adding young men to your choirs when they understand clearly that you are doing much more than just teaching songs. Give principals, counselors, and other teachers recognition on your programs and in your concerts.

You must do the legwork which recruiting demands. Talk to students in the halls. Play on the faculty sports teams. Attend student sports events. Keep your classroom open after school so that students have a place for socializing.

VII

TEACHER PRESCRIPTIONS FOR SANITY

In working with the boy's changing voice, several common problems arise. The following list offers classroom-tested solutions for dealing with these everyday occurrences.

PROBLEM: Pitch-matching for new baritones and subterranean basses

> **SOLUTION #1:** Instead of requiring that the boy match the pitch you give, allow the boy to sing a comfortable pitch and then you match his pitch in a comfortable octave for you. You want that boy to know what it "feels" like to match a pitch.

> **SOLUTION #2:** Have a fellow baritone who can match pitch sing to the non-matching friend instead of using a piano.

> **SOLUTION #3:** Exercise great patience. Give positive strokes. Find out the boy's music aptitude and use appropriate Gordon tonal syllables if he is ready for them. Boys may spend months before they are consistently successful. See Appendix IV, pages 64-67.

PROBLEM: A boy refuses to sing in the upper register.

> **SOLUTION #1:** Create a rap song which demands that the singer speak at the comfortable extremes of his voice, e.g., "I really wanna sing, I really wanna sing" (spoken on a very low pitch) -"Listen to me rap, Listen to me rap" (spoken on a very high pitch, hopefully falsetto). Tell him that if he can speak that high, he is also able to sing sounds at that pitch level, given some extra time and practice.

> **SOLUTION #2:** Say "Here, kitty, kitty" in a high voice, as if calling a cat.

> **SOLUTION #3:** Have the boy count 1-2-3-4, with 1 and 3 being spoken low and 2 and 4 spoken very high.

PROBLEM: A boy who sang for several weeks suddenly stops singing in your rehearsals. The assumption is that he has had several signs of rather rapid voice change.

> **SOLUTION:** Help him accept his voice change by first drawing him into regular class discussions, having him run errands or grade papers, thus building his self-esteem. Later, speak to him privately about what you have noticed about the change in his voice. Later still, test his voice privately and chart what has happened.

PROBLEM: You cannot locate a spring musical with an accompaniment tape which has the correct range for your male lead.

> **SOLUTION:** Rewrite the solo(s) using the teacher's manual for the harmonic progressions. Place the rewritten solo(s) in a tessitura which allows for maximum projection of the lead's voice. The flute-like quality of many Treble and Cambiata voices does not carry well and can elicit negative peer comments.

PROBLEM: Your boys do not want to participate in solo-ensemble festivals.

> **SOLUTION #1:** Adapt literature to fit the individual boys' voices rather than say that they do not have to be involved (See Chapter III). Give a copy of your adaptation to the judge with an explanation. Carefully check your state handbook for participation in music contests to avoid embarrassment for any boy.

> **SOLUTION #2:** Rather than having boys sing solos, encourage them to form small male ensembles using quality literature. They will respond positively to this challenge.

PROBLEM: Male sections cannot hold their part within an ensemble.

> **SOLUTION #1:** In your rehearsal, place chairs for the problem male sections directly in front of the piano and surround the piano with the other sections.
>
> **SOLUTION #2:** Using circle formations for each section, work difficult passages independently. As success increases, intertwine the circles with the problem male section in the center.

"We got it right this time, Ms. Emerson!"

PROBLEM: Girls become frustrated with "slow" male sections.

> **SOLUTION:** Schedule a sectional for the boys outside of class time. Provide refreshments and a recording of the Kings Singers to create atmosphere, then work the boys hard. Give strong and positive feedback.

PROBLEM: Vocal quality of baritones becomes harsh and pushed as they approach middle C.

> **SOLUTION:** Use vocalises which are five-note descending patterns. Cultivate descending scale patterns which begin in the falsetto (See Appendix III). Offer images of sighing or those which provide for a mixing of tone qualities both from falsetto and regular voice. Give more tall "space" to the vowel being sung and less pressure on the pitch. Talk about arching the tone from above, as in a basketball free throw approaching the basket. Keep the energy flowing through the tone.

VIII

SCORES THAT DON'T BORE

The following recommended works are drawn from many of the choral genre which represent our western choral heritage—oratorio choruses, cantata movements, folk song arrangements, movements from church masses, motets, madrigals, spirituals, and choral songs. All eras, Renaissance through Contemporary, are represented. Each work is graded according to level of difficulty, E (easy), M (medium), MD (medium difficult), D (difficult). The ranges for each vocal part are also given. Though important in the broad spectrum of choral literature, pop, show choir, and vocal jazz scores have not been included. You should not ignore these additional sources of music which are a part of our contemporary culture. "C" denotes "cambiata" in this compilation.

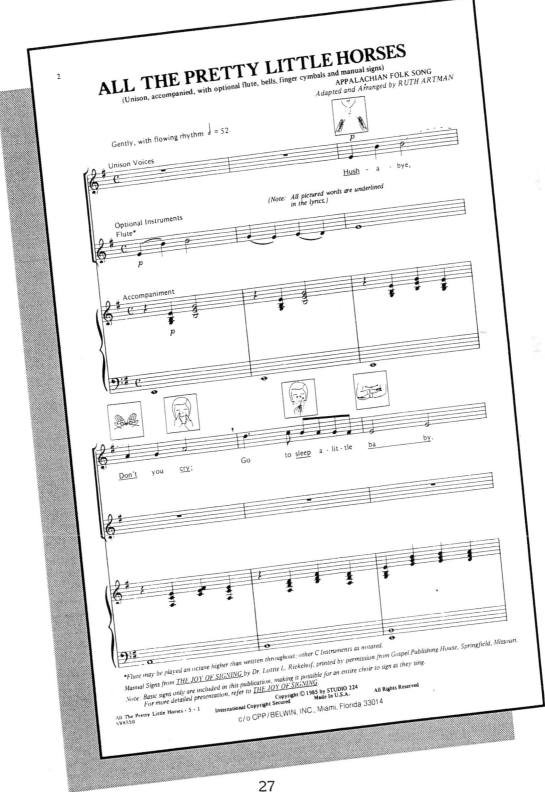

UNISON

Title	Comp./Arr.	Voicing	Publisher	Code #	Diff. Lev.	Comments
All The Pretty Little Horses	Artman	Unison	CPP/Belwin	SV8550	E	
Bandicoot	Jennings	Unison	G. Schirmer	12434	E	
Brother James' Air	Bain/Gibson	Unison	Novello	290603	E	
Eucaristica	Casals	Unison	Tetra	TCI55	D	opt. 3-pt.
Festival Alleluia	Pote	Unison	Choristers Guild	CGA 280	MD	
Guiding Star	Scott	Unison or 2-pt.	AMSI	541	M	
I Thank Thee, Lord	Paterson	Unison	Beckenhorst	BP1158	M	flute or alto recorder
Knight Music	Bailey	Unison	Kjos	6178	D	

Title	Comp./Arr.	Voicing	Publisher	Code #	Diff. Lev.	Com- ments
Never A Night Like This	Hunnicutt	Unison	C. Fischer	SG 142	M	descant
Shivery Sarah	H. Nelson	Unison	Roberton Pub.	75321	M	
Silly Sally Sue	Nelson	Unison	Boosey & Hawkes	6114	M	
The Lord's Prayer	Warner/Pfohl	Unison	Brodt Music	210	MD	
The Path To The Moon	Thiman	Unison	Boosey & Hawkes	6114	MD	
The World's End	Burtch	Unison	Roberton Pub.	312-41525	M	
We Will Sing For Joy	Scarlatti/Lowe	Unison	Choristers Guild	CGA 202	MD	
You'll Never Guess What I Saw	Henderson	Unison	Gordon Thompson Music	Gl77	MD	

TWO-PART/SA/TB

Title	Comp./Arr.	Voicing	Publisher	Code #	Diff. Lev.	Comments
Alleluia	Bach/Artman	Unison/2-part	Hal Leonard	08570202	E	
Alleluia, Sing With Joy	Perry & Perry	2-part	Shawnee Press	EA 71	M	
Am Strande	Brahms	SA	National Music	99	MD	
Ave Maria	Arcadelt/Eilers	2-part	Jenson	402-01162	M	
Awake The Trumpet's Lofty Sound	Handel/Lojeski	2-part	Hal Leonard	08401438	D	
Boots And Saddles	Tidball	2-part	Boosey & Hawkes	6118	M	
Christmas Dance Of The Shepherds	Kodály	SA	Presser	312-40573	MD	a cappella
Comic Duet For Two Cats	Rossini/Craig/ Mason	SA or TB	Plymouth	PCS 538	D	

TWO-PART/SA/TB (continued)

Title	Comp./Arr.	Voicing	Publisher	Code #	Diff. Lev.	Comments
Den Tod (from Cantata #4)	Bach/ Kochanek	2-part	Heritage	HV117	MD	tape available
Duet from Cantata No. 37 (I Will Praise the Lord)	Bach	SA	Boosey & Hawkes	OC2B 6413	D	
Go Gently Into The Morning	D. Wagner	2-part	Hinshaw	HMC942	M	
Hodie, Nobis De Caelo	A. Grandi	SA	Mark Foster	803	MD	
How Brightly Shines The Morning Star	Praetorius	2-part treble	Boosey & Hawkes	OC2B 6419	MD	a cappella
If You've Only Got A Moustache	Foster/ Van Camp	TB	Somerset	BR2011	E	
Kyrie	Klouse	2-part	Hal Leonard	08704234	MD	
Liza Jane	Scott	2-part	CPP/Belwin	SV8957	E	

Title	Comp./Arr.	Voicing	Publisher	Code #	Diff. Lev.	Comments
Maria, Mater Gratiae	Fauré	2-part	A. Broude	948	D	
No, No, Resistance Is But Vain	Purcell	SA	Presser	352-00052	D	
O Clap Your Hands	J. Butler	2-part treble	Concordia	98-2734	M	
Old Roger Is Dead	Frackenpohl	SA	Kjos	6117	MD	
Once In A Dream	Hurd	SA	Novello	160199	MD	
Praises, Let Us Sing	Mauret/Kirk	2-part	A. Broude	948	MD	opt. brass quartet parts available
Red, Red Rose	Schubert/Harris	2-part	Jenson	416-18012	M	
Reflections Of A Lad At Sea	Besig	2-part	Shawnee Press	E267	M	

Title	Comp./Arr.	Voicing	Publisher	Code #	Diff. Lev.	Comments
Sound The Trumpet! Praise Him	Haydn/Hopson	2-part	Coronet Press	CP 365	MD	opt. brass quartet available
Swell The Full Chorus	Handel/Hadley	2-part	CPP/Belwin	3024	M	
The Angel Carol	Snyder	2-part	CPP/Belwin	SV8909	M	opt. descant
The Cat Came Back	Miller/Lewis	2-part	Shawnee Press	E 320	M	solos
The Shepherd Psalm	Carter	2 equal voices	Hope	A555	M	
The Water Is Wide	Zaninelli	SA or TB	Shawnee Press	E 83	M	
Three Hungarian Folk Songs	Seiber	2-part	G. Schirmer	10826	MD	
To The Ploughboy	Vaughan Williams	SA	Oxford	385794-4	M	

Title	Comp./Arr.	Voicing	Publisher	Code #	Diff. Lev.	Com- ments
Too Many Cats (speaking only)	Keen	2-part speaking chorus	Heritage	HV117	MD	
Trains	Fitch	2-part/SC	Cambiata Press	T978117	M	
Two Bartók Songs	Bartók/Suchoff	2-part treble	Plymouth	PCS 561	MD	
Two Handel Classics	Handel/Perry & Perry	2-part	Shawnee Press	E 320	MD	
Velvet Shoes	R. Thompson	SA	E.C. Schirmer	2526	E	
Weg Der Liebe	Brahms	SA or TB	National Music	69	MD	
Wondrous Love	Collins	2-part variable	Cambiata Press	S97685	M	

THREE-PART/SSA/SSAA

Title	Comp./Arr.	Voicing	Publisher	Code #	Diff. Lev.	Comments
A Girl's Garden	R. Thompson	SAA	E.C. Schirmer	2540-5	M	
Alleluja	Mozart/ Spevacek	SSA	Jenson	437-01013	M	
Confitemini Domino	Constantini/ Kirk	3-part treble	CPP/Belwin	PROCH 03002	MD	
El Grillo (The Cricket)	Josquin	SSA	Frank Music	F-2101	M	a cappella
Hotaru Koi (Ho, Firefly)	Ogura	SSA	Ongaku No Tomo Sha Corp. (Presser)	312-41520	MD	a cappella
Lift Thine Eyes To The Mountains (from "Elijah")	Mendelssohn	SSA	CPP/Belwin	SV7918	M	a cappella
Like A Blossom	Wells	SSAA	Gentry	JG-503	MD	
O Christ, Our Hope	Distler	SSA	Novello	29 0618	MD	a cappella

Title	Comp./Arr.	Voicing	Publisher	Code #	Diff. Lev.	Comments
Plaisir D'Amour (The Joys Of Love)	Martini/ Strommen	SSA	Boosey & Hawkes	OCFB 6474	MD	
Sing We And Chant It	Morley/Davis	SSAA	E.C. Schirmer	1082	D	
Spanish Song: Vesáme Y Abraçáme	Anonymous	SSA	CPP/Belwin	SV8703	MD	*a cappella,* opt. tamb.
The Alphabet	Mozart	SSA	A. Broude	933	M	
The Lord Is Merciful (Suscepit Israel)	Bach/Craig	SSA	Plymouth	DC 204	D	
The Pasture	D. Wagner	SSA	Shawnee Press	B-513	M	
The Ship That Never Returned and Bobby Shaftoe	D. Coombes	SSA	Roberton Pub.	75211	MD	*a cappella*
Two Psalms (Cor Meum and Tu Exsurgens)	di Lasso	SSA or TTB	National Music	WHC33	MD	*a cappella*

Title	Comp./Arr.	Voicing	Publisher	Code #	Diff. Lev.	Comments
Alleluia	Mozart/Ehret	SAC	Cambiata Press	M979124	M	
Hallelujah, Amen	Handel/Taylor	SSC	Cambiata Press	M17312	M	*a cappella*
Veni Jesu	Cherubini/Weck	SAT	Somerset Press	SP 754	M	

SCB

Title	Comp./Arr.	Voicing	Publisher	Code #	Diff. Lev.	Comments
Angels We Have Heard On High	Cooper	SCB	Cambiata Press	I97678	E	
For All The Saints	Vaughan Williams/ Cooper	SCB	Cambiata Press	I978103	E	
Psalm 103	Knight	SCB	Cambiata Press	T180137	M	

THREE-PART MIXED/SAB

Title	Comp./Arr.	Voicing	Publisher	Code #	Diff. Lev.	Comments
A Celebration Of Bach	Bach/Jennings	3-part mixed	Heritage	HV 175	M	acc. tape available
Agnus Dei	Snyder	3-part mixed	CPP/Belwin	SV8817	M	
Ave Verum	Fauré/ Mansfield	3-part mixed	Heritage	HV116	M	
Benedictus	Lasso	3-part mixed	CPP/Belwin	SV8626	MD	from Doulce Memoire Mass
Blow Thy Horn, Hunter	Cornyshe	3-part mixed	CPP/Belwin	SV8638	M	
Canon (fuga a tre)	Praetorious	SAB	CPP/Belwin	SV8569	E	*a cappella*
Domine Deus	Regnart	SAB	CPP/Belwin	SV8845	MD	*a cappella*
Free I Am Once Again (Nun Bin Ich Einmal Frei)	Regnart	SAB	CPP/Belwin	SV8615	M	*a cappella*

Title	Comp./Arr.	Voicing	Publisher	Code #	Diff. Lev.	Comments
Gloria	Corteccia	3-part mixed	CPP/Belwin	SV9021	M	16th century
Gloria In Excelsis	Haydn/Ehret	SAB	European American	EA 383	M	from "Heilig-messe"
Good Christian Men, Rejoice	Covert	3-part variable	Cambiata Press	U 97561	E	
Grant Us Peace	Scott	SAB	CPP/Belwin	SV9015	E	
Hosanna In Excelsis	di Lasso	SAB	CPP/Belwin	SV8613	M	*a cappella*
I Got A Robe	Willet	3-part mixed	Heritage	HV170	E	acc. tape available
Je Ne Fus Jamais Si Aise (The Sound Of Pipe And Drum)	Certon	SAB	CPP/Belwin	SV8935	D	16th century French
Joshua Fit The Battle Of Jericho	Willet	3-part mixed	Heritage	HV108	E	

Title	Comp./Arr.	Voicing	Publisher	Code #	Diff. Lev.	Comments
Kyrie	Klouse	SAB	Hal Leonard	08704233	M	piano acc.
Lift Thine Eyes (from "Elijah")	Mendelssohn/ Kirby	3-part variable	Cambiata Press	M 117322	M	*a cappella*
Make A Joyful Noise	L. Walter	3-part mixed	CPP/Belwin	SV8642	M	
O My Heart	Henry VIII	SAB	CPP/Belwin	SV8817	E	*a cappella*, opt. strings or recorder
On Christmas Night	Artman	3-part mixed	CPP/Belwin	SV8916	M	18th cent. Eng. carol
Pat-A-Pan	Krone	3-part variable	Kjos	ED 6185	E	opt. auto-harp
Plenty Good Room	Horman	3-part	Somerset Press	SP 815	E	small group
Praise The Lord (from "Judas Maccabeus")	Handel/Hopson	SAB	H. Flammer	D 5225	D	

THREE-PART MIXED/SAB (continued)

Title	Comp./Arr.	Voicing	Publisher	Code #	Diff. Lev.	Comments
Rosebud In June	Davis	3-part mixed	CPP/Belwin	SV8925	E	a cappella opt. hand drum & recorder
Shenandoah	Spevacek	3-part mixed	Jenson	437-19040	M	opt. solo
Sing To God	Viadana/ Coggin	SAB	Presser	312-41451	D	
Spanish Song: Vesáme Y Abraçáme	Anonymous	3-part mixed	CPP/Belwin	SV8704	M	a cappella, opt. tamb.
Strike It Up, Tabor	Weelkes	3-part mixed	CPP/Belwin	SV8639	MD	16th century canzonetta
The Angel Carol	Snyder	3-part mixed	CPP/Belwin	SV8908	M	familiar French carol
The Heavens Declare (from "Joshua")	Handel/Ross	SAB	Presser	392-41450	M	
The Pain Of Love (Ach Gott, Ein Grosse Pein)	Regnart	3-part mixed	CPP/Belwin	SV8630	M	a cappella

Title	Comp./Arr.	Voicing	Publisher	Code #	Diff. Lev.	Comments
The Road Not Taken	Klouse	SAB	Hal Leonard	08704934	M	Robert Frost poem
The Sound Of The Sea	M. Wilson	3-part mixed	Kimmel Publications	1217-319	M	
Three Spirituals For Changing Voices	Thygerson	SAT or SATB	Heritage	H6509	M	
We Be Three Poor Mariners	Ravenscroft	SAB	CPP/Belwin	SV8569	E	*a cappella*
Who Has Seen The Wind?	Snyder	3-part mixed	CPP/Belwin	SV8728	E	Rossetti poem

SATB/SACB/SSAB/SSCB

Title	Comp./Arr.	Voicing	Publisher	Code #	Diff. Lev.	Com-ments
Adoramus Te	Palestrina/ Farrell	SSCB	Cambiata Press	M485187	E	*a cappella*
Agnus Dei	Gabrieli/ McCray	SACB	Cambiata Press	M97682	MD	*a cappella*
Agnus Dei	Hassler	SATB	CPP/Belwin	SV8918	MD	*a cappella*
Alleluia	Mozart/Daniels	SATB	Presser	392-41469	M	
Ave Verum	Mozart/Lyle	SSCB	Cambiata Press	M17552	MD	
Ave Verum Corpus	Byrd/Collins	SSCB	Cambiata Press	D978121	MD	*a cappella*
Carol Of The Bells	Leontovich/ Knight	SSCB	Cambiata Press	U983176	E	*a cappella*
Come All Ye Fair And Tender Ladies	Collins	SSC(B)	Cambiata Press	ARS 980152	E	

44

Title	Comp./Arr.	Voicing	Publisher	Code #	Diff. Lev.	Comments
Coventry Carol	Durham	SATB	Deseret Music	DEM3009	E	opt. flute
Festival Sanctus	Leavitt	SATB	CPP/Belwin	SV8821	D	mixed meters
Fiddler Man	Rutter	SATB	Hinshaw	HMC 815	D	
Flow Not So Fast Ye Fountains	Dowland/ Thoburn	SSAB	CPP/Belwin	OCT 02558	M	*a cappella*
Gloria	Vivaldi/Collins	SSCB	Cambiata Press	M117207	MD	
Gloria (from First Mass in B-flat)	Hummel	SATB	Walton	WW1024	D	
Gloria In Excelsis	Lotti/Livingston	SATB	Presser	392-41353	MD	
Gloria In Excelsis Deo	L. Walter	SATB	CPP/Belwin	SV8735	MD	Latin text

SATB/SACB/SSAB/SSCB (continued)

Title	Comp./Arr.	Voicing	Publisher	Code #	Diff. Lev.	Comments
Gloria In Excelsis Deo	Snyder	SSAB	CPP/Belwin	SV8820	M	
Go Tell It On The Mountain	Springfield	SSCB	Cambiata Press	S117325	M	
God Rest Ye Merry, Gentlemen	Lovelace	SACB	Cambiata Press	C117324	M	
Hallelujah (Messiah)	Handel/ Richison	4-part variable	Cambiata Press	M97317	D	
Hark All Ye Lovely Saints	Weelkes	SSAB	CPP/Belwin	SV8913	MD	a cappella
He Watching Over Israel (from "Elijah")	Mendelssohn/ Collins	SSCB	Cambiata Press	M97557	MD	
Hosanna	Gregor/Lyle	Double Chorus (SA-SSCB)	Cambiata Press	M979135	M	
Hush! Somebody's Callin' My Name	Dennard	SATB	Shawnee Press	A-1802	M	solo

46

Title	Comp./Arr.	Voicing	Publisher	Code #	Diff. Lev.	Comments
Introit and Kyrie (Requiem)	Fauré/ Kicklighter	SSCB	Cambiata Press	M117692	MD	
Jan Waselu	Leontovich	SATB	Shawnee Press	A 540	M	*a cappella*
Jesu Priceless Treasure (Chorale from the Motet)	Bach	SSCB	Cambiata Press	M982170	M	*a cappella*
Kyrie	Leavitt	SATB	CPP/Belwin	SV8904	M	
Lovers Love The Spring	Frackenpohl	SATB	E.B. Marks	00007758	M	Shakespeare text
Mon Coeur Se Recommande	Lasso/Porter	SATB	Alfred	6885	M	French chanson (Eng. also)
Music When Soft Voices Die	E. Butler	SATB	AMSI	1017	MD	
My Lord What A Morning	Knight	SSCB	Cambiata Press	S485185	M	*a cappella*

Title	Comp./Arr.	Voicing	Publisher	Code #	Diff. Lev.	Comments
Non e Tempo	Cara	SATB	European American	EA119	MD	*a cappella*
O Magnum Mysterium	Victoria	SSAB	Jenson	402-15080	D	*a cappella*
O Mortal Man	McCray	SSAACBB	New Music Co.	NM 147	M	*a cappella*
O Rest In The Lord (Elijah)	Mendelssohn/ Knight	SSCB	Cambiata Press	M117567	MD	
Prayer Of St. Francis	Pote	SATB	Hinshaw	888	M	
Rain, Rain	Maslanka	SATB	Kjos	ED GC142	E	*a cappella*
Ride The Chariot	Thomas	SATB	Hinshaw	HMC 931	D	opt. conga drum
Sing No More Of Sadness	Praetorius/ Spevacek	SSAB	Jenson	437-19180	M	from Terpsichore (1612)

Title	Comp./Arr.	Voicing	Publisher	Code #	Diff. Lev.	Comments
Swing Low, Sweet Chariot	Kirby	SAT(C)B	Cambiata Press	S17555	M	
The First Snow Of Winter	Leaf	SATB	Kjos	ED 8634	D	*a cappella*
The Star Spangled Banner	Collins	SSCB	Cambiata Press	D978123	E	
Three Sacred Christmas Songs	Collins	4-part	Cambiata Press	MP983171	M	
When Rooks Fly Homeward	Baynon	SATB	Boosey & Hawkes	1870	M	*a cappella*
Younger Generation	Copland/Swift	SATB	Boosey & Hawkes	1723	MD	

THREE PART/CCB BOYS

Title	Comp./Arr.	Voicing	Publisher	Code #	Diff. Lev.	Comments
Alleluia	Bach/Siltman	CCB	Cambiata Press	M486198	E	
Boatmen Stomp	Gray	3-part	G. Schirmer	12396	E	
Come, Ye Sons Of Art	Land	TTB	Plymouth	PCS 308	MD	
Down The River	Green	CCB	Cambiata Press	U485182	M	
Li'l Liza Jane	Swenson	CCB	Cambiata Press	U979134	M	
O Sing Unto The Lord	Swenson	CCB	Cambiata Press	S982163	MD	
Scarborough Fair	Swenson	CCB	Cambiata Press	U97691	E	
Sing Me A Song Of A Lad That Is Gone	Porterfield	TTB	CPP/Belwin	SV9003	M	Robert L. Stevenson text

Title	Comp./Arr.	Voicing	Publisher	Code #	Diff. Lev.	Com- ments
The Holly And The Ivy	Collins	CCB	Cambiata Press	L97688	E	
Viva Tutti	Anon/Hunter	TTB	Lawson-Gould	778	MD	

THREE PART/CBB BOYS

Title	Comp./Arr.	Voicing	Publisher	Code #	Diff. Lev.	Com- ments
A Sea Song	Swenson	CBB	Cambiata Press	C981158	MD	
America	Carey/Siltman	CBB	Cambiata Press	P486197	M	
America, The Beautiful	Ward/Siltman	CBB	Cambiata Press	P980147	M	
Fairest Lord Jesus	Siltman	CBB	Cambiata Press	U983180	E	*a cappella*
Home On That Rock	K. Shaw	TBB	Hal Leonard	08657754	D	*a cappella*
Jesu, Joy Of Man's Desiring	Bach/Siltman	CBB	Cambiata Press	M97687	M	
Oh, Won't You Sit Down?	Lawrence	CBB	Cambiata Press	U982162	E	
Spiritual Trilogy	Siltman	CBB	Cambiata Press	S980148	MD	

THREE PART/CBB BOYS (continued)

Title	Comp./Arr.	Voicing	Publisher	Code #	Diff. Lev.	Comments
Three Christmas Carols	Swenson	CBB	Cambiata Press	U979133	E	
Vive L'Amour	Siltman	CBB	Cambiata Press	U980146	MD	
Who Came To See?	Baker	CBB	Cambiata Press	C485181	M	

FOUR PART/CCBB/TTBB BOYS

Title	Comp./Arr.	Voicing	Publisher	Code #	Diff. Lev.	Comments
Ave Maria	Arcadelt/ Johnstone	CCBB	Cambiata Press	M97442	D	*a cappella*
Integer Vitae	Flemming	CCBB	Cambiata Press	M97562	E	*a cappella*
Old Man Noah Knew A Thing Or Two	Wadsworth/ Bock	TTBB	Gentry	JG 232	MD	*a cappella*
The Sea Is Now Calling	Koepke	TTBB	CPP/Belwin	SV8846	MD	opt. flute/ recorder
Together We'll Make The Journey	Beal	CCBB/Brass	Cambiata Press	L97563	E	*a cappella*

COLLECTIONS AND LARGER WORKS

Title	Comp./Arr.	Voicing	Publisher	Code #	Diff. Lev.	Comments
A Little Cantata (Ten Traditional Rhymes)	Harries	SA & Piano	Oxford University Press		D	
Classics For Two	Emerson	2-part	Jenson	403-0337	M	acc. tape available
Familiar Christmas Carols For Changing Voices (10 Carols)	Hardin		Cambiata Press		E	

IX

CONCLUSION

Working with adolescent boys may be challenging, but it is also a great privilege. If you try the ideas in this manual, your reward will be the looks on the faces of young men who have come through a semester or two of vocal change with confidence and greater self-esteem. They will recruit for you. They will volunteer for the big and the little things that need to be done in your choral area. They won't forget that you challenged them to sing falsetto when they had never tried it before. They won't forget that you also made singing a deeply rewarding activity because they experienced success - Oh, what an important word! - success in singing tonal patterns, understanding a sixteenth-century Latin motet text, reading notes, singing a one-line solo well during rehearsal, discovering diaphragmatic breathing, conducting the class in a vocalise or checking the class roll for one week.

Today, more than ever before, the fine arts are in need of teachers like you who will try new ideas or refine old ones, who love daily interaction with these young men, these "diamonds in the rough." You can teach so that music will touch the hearts and minds of young men as they move through puberty. They will want to continue singing for the rest of their lives because of special moments of self-revelation that happened to them in your rehearsals. You can go far beyond just coping with changing voices. You can help mold lives full of hope and the joy of living.

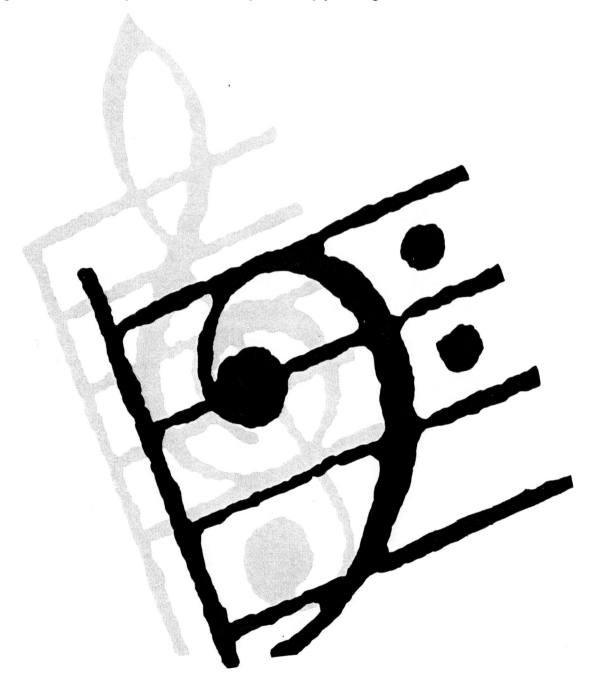

APPENDIX I

BREATHING AND POSTURE

1. Breath Actuator

sh   sh   sh   sh   shoo   (shee, sheh, shoh, shah)

2. Belt-level (Diaphragmatic) Expansion With Inhalation

Lie on the floor on your back. Place a book on your belly button area. Take in air slowly as if you are sucking through a straw so that you gently lift the book several inches. Exhale by softly and rapidly repeating the ABC's without pause until all air is expelled. The book will descend. Repeat the process. Have a contest.

When the above breathing approach begins to work, see if you can sit on a chair or stand and achieve the same expansion.

3. Slow, Controlled Exhalation With Expanded Rib Cage

While standing erect with arms up and hands interlocked and touching the top of your head, practice constant, soft s-s-s-s-s-s sounds. Let air slowly escape like from a bicycle tire. Keep your rib cage expanded as if you are holding up a round barrel that is the same size as your chest at almost its fullest expanded position.

"You want me to do WHAT?"

4. Quick Inhalation and Quick Exhalation Awareness

Stand "tall" with the rib cage expanded. At a moderate tempo, alternate counting two beats with a pig-like snort through your nose for inhalation: "1, 2," snort (like a pig!), "3, 4," snort, "5, 6," snort, "7, 8," snort! Your belly button area should expand outward as the snort causes belt-level inhalation. Everyone will laugh when you introduce this exercise, but it works.

At a moderate tempo, alternate counting two beats with a loudly spoken "hey" for exhalation: "1, 2," hey, "3, 4," hey, "5, 6," hey, "7, 8," hey! Your belly button area should contract as the "hey" causes belt-level exhalation. Say the "hey" both with the chest voice (like a shout) and the falsetto voice (or high head voice for your girls).

5. Physical Awakening

Alternate one minute of jumping jacks with one minute of slow, fluid, sweeping vertical arm motions starting at one's face or mid-body. Trace an arc with the outstretched fingers of each hand. Hands may move together or independently.

6. Tension Reduction Exercises

While standing in a body position of alertness, do, in any order, slow head rolls, side bends, sky reaches, shoulder rolls, jaw flops, windshield wiper eyebrows, mouth openers, half-body forward flops, and deep knee bends. With any number of body appendages, mime different mental scenes: a spring breeze, a thunderstorm, a sprinkling rain, wind blowing a sheet on a clothesline, an elegant Mozart minuet, or an expressive teenager looking at a beautiful sunset.

TONE QUALITY

1. Forward Focus With Resonance In Head (Eyes, Cheeks, Nose, Forehead)

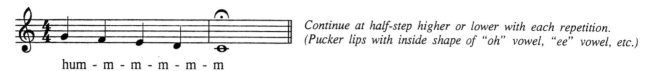

hum - m - m - m - m - m

Continue at half-step higher or lower with each repetition.
(Pucker lips with inside shape of "oh" vowel, "ee" vowel, etc.)

2. Tall "oo" Vowel With Inside Space

Put tip of straightened index finger on nose (as if you are going to say, "shh!") while tilting bottom of hand slightly away from your mouth. Pucker your lips around an *oo* vowel and then touch your index finger with your lips at the middle joint of your finger. Be sure to keep your jaw free and floating by moving it back and forth as you touch your finger with the lips. Open to an oval, fish-mouth shape and place an imaginary toothpick in a vertical position inside your mouth. Siren from low pitches to very high pitches with a "hoo, hoo, hoo." Say "Who Are You?" using the puckered *oo* vowel on the first and last words. Sing, in falsetto voice, the same phrase. Keep jaw loose!

3. Basic Vowels and The Vowel Wheel

Speak each vowel in this "wheel" with the "toothpick-tall" inside space until the distinctions between vowels are clearly discernible by others. On long tones, sing several vowels which are close to one another on the wheel. Sing vowels which are not contiguous. Have students tape record themselves at school for listening to themselves at home. In a legato manner, sing all vowels on the wheel on one comfortable pitch using energized breath.

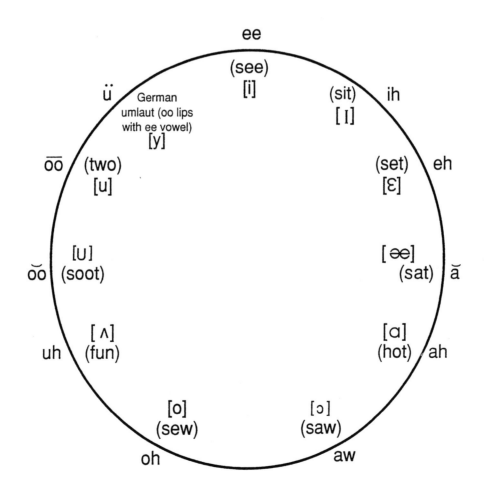

4. Vowel Unification With Breath Management

Start with a "puckered lips" *oo* vowel (a doughnut mouth) for the first pattern, then sing the same pattern on an *ee* vowel through the same puckered lips. Keep jaw loose by moving it laterally. Drop the jaw slightly for the *eh* vowel; round your lips for the *oh;* drop the jaw a bit more for the *ah* vowel. Try singing this entire vowel cycle, *oo, ee, eh, oh, ah,* on one "book-lifting" breath.

oo - - - - ee - - - - eh - - - - oh - - - - ah.

5. Forward Focus Using Closed "NG" Sound

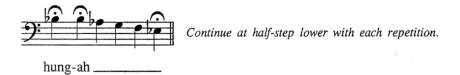

Continue at half-step lower with each repetition.

hung-ah _____

APPENDIX III

RANGE DEVELOPMENT AND FLEXIBILITY

1. Register Development and Connection For Boys' Changing Voices

a. In falsetto and at the **actual notated pitches,** repeat the pattern below at successively lower half steps without letting the voice change to the heavier speaking quality. Sing as low as possible. Keep jaw loose and breath flowing. After months (or possibly years) of daily practice, be alert to the possible emergence of a slightly weightier "mixed" register that will bridge over what were once "breaks" in the voice.

Continue at half-step lower with each repetition.

coo coo coo coo coo

b. Do the same exercise above but let the lower register change happen when it seems comfortable to the individual. These "breaks," changes from one set of muscles to another in the larynx, or "gear shifts," occur at different pitch levels for different boys. The pitches at which the "breaks" occur can be grouped into two general areas: (a) b, c^1, $c\#^1$, d^1, and (b) e^1, f^1, $f\#^1$, g^1.

Register changes are a natural adjustment in the vocal mechanism. With patient, proper practice and sufficient time, young male singers can develop a seamless voice in which the high register melds into the mixed register before joining smoothly with the low register. Be sure to maintain the warm vowel sound in these exercises which may be used over a period of years.

2. Low To High Pattern With Closed To Open Vowels

Sing at a rapid tempo with loose jaw, active lips, and tall vowels in a rhythmic style with quick, "surprise," breaths between each repeat of the pattern.

Continue at half-step higher with each repetition.

sing   a   song. _____

3. Low Register To Falsetto To Low Register Glissando

Sing or speak "I" in low register. Siren from high pitch downward as if you were falling off the Grand Canyon in slow motion. Siren (do not sing) across any register breaks. Keep jaw and neck loose as you slide. Do not be concerned about "blank spots," strange noises, or blatant shifts of register. Accept them as temporary and harmless.

I   saw   you!

4. Efficient Use Of Breath With Pitch Agility

Sing with a gentle staccato. Touch the pitches with a velvet glove rather than "hitting" them with hammer-like strokes. Alternate with legato style.

Continue at half-step higher with each repetition.

hoo - - - heh - - - ha - - - - -

61

5. Low To High Scale Pattern

Begin by singing at slow tempi. Keep the vowels focused forward in the face, eyes, and cheeks with tall inside space.

Continue at half-step higher with each repetition (oo, oh, etc.)

ah

6. Consonant Clarity Exercises

Speak, chant, and sing the following sentences. Create short melodic motives. Use lips, mouth, jaw, tongue, eyes, and face with complete abandon for achieving freedom and clarity. Try dramatizing the sentences in different, even extreme, parts of the voice range. Keep the torso supple and free. Watch carefully for subtle tightening of the jaw. Stop the exercise if you can tell that a student's jaw is becoming tense.

As the students master the consonant combinations, pay careful attention to the shape and sound of the vowels and diphthongs. Analyze the various challenges in these exercises. Try accents, e.g., British, U.S. Bronx, Deep South, Oklahoma-Texas Twang, etc.

   a. Bright dawns the blinding new day.
   b. Can good kings control current clashes?
   c. How hopeful we were when handling white whales.
   d. Rubber baby buggy bumpers!
   e. Put bad pennies back in black pots.
   f. Join cheerfully in jeering zealous pleasure seekers.
   g. Mommy made me mash my M & M's!
   h. Bumble, Bumble, Bumble Bee!
   i. Help me wash and wax my white Winnebago.

   j. To sit in solemn silence in a dull, dark, dock, in a pestilential prison with a life-long lock, awaiting the sensation of a short, sharp, shock, from a cheap and chippy chopper on a big, black, block! (Gilbert and Sullivan, THE MIKADO)

"Aren't you listening? She said Fortissimo!"

APPENDIX IV

EAR TRAINING

1. Awareness Of Dynamic Levels and Balance Between Parts

At varying tempi, sing this exercise on "loo," "lah," or "lee." The half-note accompaniment part can be sung on "bmm" or any vowel. Note the effect of the darker *(oo)* and brighter vowel *(ee)* timbres on tuning and on the different dynamic levels. Have students change parts. Sing the written bass line an octave higher. Have one part sing one dynamic level louder than all others. Transpose to more appropriate keys if needed. Improvise melodies over this two-chord exercise. Add additional parts which harmonize with the tonic (I) and dominant (V) chords.

2. Octave Displacement Practice

Before introducing written changes in the music (to fit boys' ranges), begin teaching octave displacement during vocalises. Once an established displacement jump has been learned, change the vocalise to fit current music needs. You can use numbers or solfege syllables, depending on your personal preference.

Transpose to fit boys' individual needs.

do	re	mi	fa	so	la	ti	do	ti	la	so	fa	mi	re	do
1	2	3	4	5	6	7	8	7	6	5	4	3	2	1

3. Gordon Tonal and Rhythm Syllables

Ear training is a must in every choral rehearsal. Tonal and rhythm patterns are primary tools in teaching ear training and music reading. Just as in language we derive meaning through the organization of words, so in music we derive musical meaning through the organization of tonal and rhythmic patterns. [17]

Tonal patterns establish major, minor, and modal tonality. Tonal patterns also define keyality: C, C♯, D, etc. Rhythm patterns establish meter - duple, triple, etc. - and, consequently, tempo. Tonal and rhythmic patterns are the foundation for expression, form, style, dynamics, and timbre in music. [18]

Below are listed the first three parts of Gordon's Tonal Unit 1 (Figures 8, 9, and 10). [19] Tonal Unit 1, Section A, Criterion 1 is the first of a research-based, carefully planned sequence of 42 Tonal Units. With it, you can begin the ear training portion of your rehearsal warm-ups.

Before using these patterns in class, become acquainted with any new terminology, how the Tonal Units are used, what to expect from your choir as you begin using patterns, and how to test for your students' music aptitude. [20] Space does not permit a complete explanation of Gordon's Learning Sequence Activities which contain all the patterns of the Tonal and Rhythm Units. However, an introduction to the Tonal Units is offered here. [21]

As noted on page 22, Gordon's tonal and rhythm patterns are most effective when used for five to ten minutes each day. Use tonal patterns every other rehearsal one week, rhythm patterns every other rehearsal the next week if you want maximum long-term results. This approach promotes a feeling of continuity from one class session to the next and keeps to a minimum any confusion between the two types of patterns.

Figure 8 (Tonal Unit 1, Section A, Criterion 1) contains four brief instructions and three tonal patterns, all of which are built on a D major triad. The tonal patterns are written at three levels of difficulty - easy (E), moderately difficult (M), and difficult (D) - to meet the needs of your students, who will demonstrate either low, average, or high tonal music aptitude.

Figure 8.

TONAL UNIT 1   SECTION A   CRITERION 1

Grade _____ Teacher _____ Date _____ Test _____

Sing tonal sequence in D major using "bum."
Sing class patterns in D major using "bum."

Teacher sings pattern using "bum."
Students sing only first pitch using "bum."

Start by singing on "bum" a series of pitches, such as 5-6-5-4-3-2-7-1 (so-la-so-fa-mi-re-ti-do), to set up the D major tonality for your class. Then make up an easy two-or three-note tonic triad pattern which will serve as the class pattern. Have your students **sing back only the first tone** of that class pattern. Then sing the first of the three written tonal patterns, the "easy" one (E), and have an individual student sing back only the first tone. **You must sing the correct pitch with each individual** so that he or she will experience success. Be sure to allow time between patterns for student audiation. Continue this process of alternation between the class singing the patterns and individuals singing them. When approximately 80% of the students have completed the patterns of Criterion 1 without your assistance, move on to Criterion 2 (Figure 9).

Figure 9.

TONAL UNIT 1   SECTION A   CRITERION 2

Grade _____ Teacher _____ Date _____ Test _____

Sing tonal sequence in D major using "bum."
Sing class patterns in D major using "bum."

Teacher sings pattern using "bum."
Students sing only resting tone using "bum."

When approximately 80% of your students have mastered the requirements for Criterion 2, move on to Criterion 3 (Figure 10).

Figure 10.

TONAL UNIT 1   SECTION A   CRITERION 3

Grade _____ Teacher _____ Date _____ Test _____

Sing tonal sequence in D major using "bum."
Sing class patterns in D major using "bum."

Teacher sings pattern using "bum."
Students sing pattern using "bum."

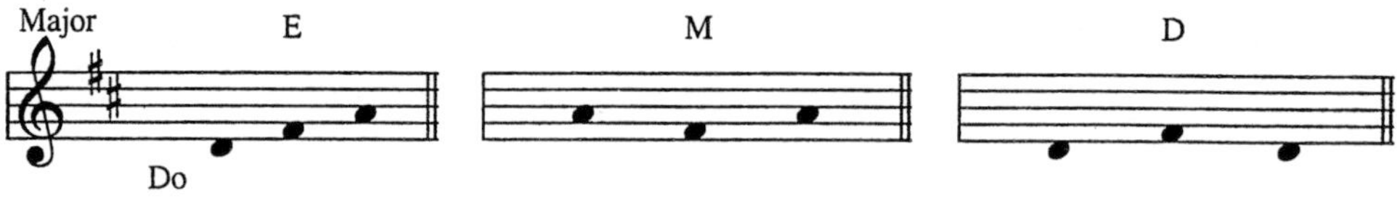

Regardless of the age of your students, start the ear training with Tonal Unit 1. [22] Sequential use of the Tonal Units is important.

1. For a starter kit, purchase the Tonal Register, Book One, Revised Edition (21 Tonal Units like Figures 8, 9, and 10). The 21 Tonal Units in Book One contain patterns in major, minor, mixolydian, and dorian modes. This book could suffice for four semesters in your choir class.

2. From whatever point you begin, teach all units and all sections sequentially - E (easy) patterns before M (moderately difficult) patterns, Unit 1 before Unit 2, and Criterion 1 before Criterion 2.

3. Use only one criterion per day to avoid confusion. Remember, you want to pave the way for success, not frustration. All students, regardless of aptitude levels, should first sing "easy" patterns before moving to moderately difficult and difficult patterns.

4. Avoid moving systematically down a row of singers and asking each person to sing. *Your goal is to have students audiate pitches silently before they actually see the printed notes.* If a student knows that he or she is next, the anxiety factor may be so high that any response may be impossible.

5. Reviewing old material is unnecessary. You will be surprised at how eager your students are to be successful and to meet the challenges inherent in these patterns.

A reminder: You may experience limited success with your students if you use these patterns without having determined your students' individual music aptitudes. Unwittingly, you will frustrate low aptitude individuals and bore high aptitude types by asking them to sing the wrong patterns.

Low music aptitude students should do well with all "easy" patterns in the Tonal Units. Average music aptitude students will be successful with the "E" and "M" patterns. High aptitude students will do well with all three patterns. Take the time and funds needed to give the ADVANCED MEASURES OF MUSIC AUDIATION, a twenty-minute aptitude test [23], if you are working with students in the seventh grade or above.

The patterns used in Tonal Unit 1, Section A (Figures 8, 9, and 10) may seem simple to you. However, you may find that many of your students need encouragement and understanding. Don't be surprised if several of the students are unable to echo accurately the first tone of an easy pattern. They may still be in what Gordon calls the "babble" stage of development, a term used to describe the stage in which a person cannot audiate and sing back "do," the home base pitch, after hearing a simple pattern.

If this happens, have the student say "hello" to you. Find the pitch or pitches on the piano. Use the Tonal Unit 1, Criterion 1 tonal pattern (two pitches) which is designed for students with low tonal music aptitude (under the E in Figure 8). Transpose it to their "hello" speaking pitch. Be patient. Give encouragement and many positive strokes when a student sings back anything on his "hello" pitch.

USING GORDON TONAL SYLLABLES:
A BRIEF OUTLINE FOR TONAL UNIT 1, SECTION A, CRITERION 1 (Figure 8)

1. Set up a tonality on a neutral syllable (bum): 5-6-5-4-3-2-7-1 (so-la-so-fa-mi-re-ti-do in major).

2. Create and then sing a two-or three-note class pattern using either a tonic or dominant triad. *All students should sing back just the first tone of the pattern you sang.* Have the class, in unison, sing the first tone of one or two other class patterns on "bum."

3. Then have an individual student echo the first tone of the "easy" pattern (d to f♯) that you sing on "bum" (Figure 8). IMPORTANT: Sing the first tone of the pattern *with the student.*

4. Return to one or two class patterns, singing each on "bum." Have the class echo the first tone of each pattern.

5. Sing the "easy" pattern. Have another student sing back only the first tone. Sing with the student as he or she sings the first tone of the pattern.

6. Selectively return to individual students who have been successful. Sing the "E" (easy) pattern. Have each student sing the first tone alone with no help from you.

7. Alternate two or three unison class patterns with the "easy" pattern sung by an individual. Remember: Do the Learning Sequence Activities (the patterns) in small doses every other rehearsal for no more than five or ten minutes. Use only one criterion, like the patterns in Figure 8, each day.

8. When about 80% of the class has been successful with Tonal Unit 1, Section A, Criterion 1, move to Tonal Unit 1, Section A, Criterion 2. Use the same procedures noted above.

When you have completed this structured process, you will have used only a portion of one Tonal Unit in a sequence of many developed by Gordon for use in general music classes, bands, orchestras, and choirs. There is a series of sequenced rhythm patterns which should be used concurrently with the tonal patterns. [24]

You are the key to the effective use of the tonal patterns. When used faithfully, these ear training exercises will lead your students successfully through the stages of music learning. Your singers will develop musical independence and pride in themselves.

The payoff is that young men and women who have trouble matching pitch will overcome that challenge and move on to greater music literacy, reading notation, and music enjoyment. Students with high music aptitude will flourish because they are challenged. They will not as likely drop out of music ensembles. Low aptitude students will also experience success, a commodity greatly needed in the youth of today.

ENDNOTES

[1]   Irvin Cooper and Karl O. Kuersteiner, **Teaching Junior High School Music**, (Conway, Arkansas: Cambiata Press, 1973).

[2]   Frederick J. Swanson, **Music Teaching in the Junior High and Middle School**, (Englewood Cliffs, New Jersey: Prentice-Hall, Inc., 1973).

[3]   Duncan McKenzie, **Training the Boy's Changing Voice**, (New Brunswick, New Jersey: Rutgers University Press, 1956), pp. 30-32.

[4]   John M. Cooksey, "The Development of a Contemporary, Eclectic Theory for the Training and Cultivation of the Junior High School Male Changing Voice," **The Choral Journal**, (October 1977 - January 1978).

[5]   John M. Cooksey, Ralph Beckett, and Richard Wiseman, "A Longitudinal Investigation of Selected Behavioral, Physiological and Acoustical Factors Associated with Voice Mutation in the Junior High School Male Adolescent," Report to the Wisconsin Music Educators Conference, University of Wisconsin, Madison, Wisconsin, October, 1980, p. 3.

[6]   Ibid., p. 2.

[7]   Ibid., pp. 3-4.

[8]   Wesley S. Coffman, "A Study of the Incidence and Characteristics of Boys' Voice Change in Grades Four, Five, and Six, and Implications for School Music Materials Deriving Therefrom," (Ph.D. dissertation, Florida State University, 1968).

[9]   Cooksey, "The Development of a Contemporary. . . ," December, 1977, pp. 8-9.

[10] Wallace Long, Jr., Notes from Choral Leadership Workshop, Emporia State University, Emporia, Kansas, October, 1988.

[11] Edwin E. Gordon, Notes from Sugarloaf Seminar on Music Learning Theory, Temple University, July, 1989.

[12] Edwin E. Gordon, **Learning Sequences in Music: Skill, Content, and Patterns**, Revised Edition, (Chicago: G.I.A. Publishers, Inc., 1989).

[13] Ibid.

[14] Edwin E. Gordon and David G. Woods, **Reference Handbook for Using Learning Sequence Activities**, Revised Edition, (Chicago: G.I.A. Publishers, Inc., 1990); discusses how and when to use the tonal and rhythm patterns.

[15] Philip S. Dale, **Language Development — Structure and Function**, (Chicago: Holt, Rinehart and Winston, 1976), p. 18.

[16] Edwin E. Gordon, **Advanced Measures of Music Audiation**, (Chicago: G.I.A. Publishers, Inc., 1989).

[17] Edwin E. Gordon and David G. Woods, **Why Use Learning Sequence Activities?** (Chicago: G.I.A. Publishers, Inc., 1985), p. 7.

[18] Ibid. p. 7.

[19] Edwin E. Gordon and David G. Woods, **Tonal Register, Book One**, Revised Edition (Chicago: G.I.A. Publishers, Inc., 1990).

[20] For a complete explanation and introduction, see Darrel L. Walters, **Learning Sequence Activities Introductory Manual**, (Chicago: G.I.A. Publishers, Inc., 1987). Our brief discussion is based on his clear, concise explanations.

[21] For help in applying Learning Sequence Activities specifically to the junior high/middle school level, see articles by Bertaux, "Teaching Children of All Ages to Use the Singing Voice" and "How To Work With Out-of-Tune Singers;" Harper, "Specific Techniques for Teaching Learning Sequence Activities;" Wierson, "The Application of Music Learning Theory to the Teaching of Middle School General Music;" and Jordan, "Music Learning Theory Applied to Choral Performance Groups," in **Readings in Music Learning Theory**, Darrel L. Walters and Cynthia Crump Taggart, eds., (Chicago: G.I.A. Publishers, Inc., 1989), pp. 92-104, 113-128, 154-167, 168-182.

[22] Darrel L. Walters, **Learning Sequence Activities Introductory Manual**, (Chicago: G.I.A. Publishers, Inc., 1987), p. 12.

[23] Gordon, **Advanced Measures of Music Audiation**

[24] Edwin E. Gordon and David G. Woods, **Rhythm Register, Book One**, Revised Edition (Chicago, G.I.A. Publishers, Inc., 1990).

SELECTED BIBLIOGRAPHY

Adcock, Eva. "The Changing Voice — The Middle/Junior High Challenge." **The Choral Journal** (October 1987): 9-11.

Barresi, Anthony. **Barresi On Adolescent Voice.** Madison, Wisconsin: UW-Videotapes, 1989. (Videotape)

Bertaux, Betty, "Teaching Children of All Ages to Use the Singing Voice," and "How to Work with Out-of-Tune Singers." **Readings in Music Learning Theory.** Darrel L. Walters and Cynthia Crump Taggart, eds. Chicago: G.I.A. Publishers, Inc., 1989, 92-104.

Coffman, Wesley S. "A Study of the Incidence and Characteristics of Boys' Voice Change in Grades Four, Five, and Six, and Implications for School Music Materials Deriving Therefrom." Unpublished doctoral dissertation, Florida State University, 1968.

Collins, Don L. "The Changing Voice — The High School Challenge." **The Choral Journal** (October 1987): 13-17.

Cooksey, John M. "The Development of a Contemporary, Eclectic Theory for the Training and Cultivation of the Junior High School Male Changing Voice." **The Choral Journal** (October 1977 - January 1978).

Cooksey, John M., Beckett, Ralph, and Wiseman, Richard. "A Longitudinal Investigation of Selected Behavioral, Physiological and Acoustical Factors Associated with Voice Mutation in the Junior High School Male Adolescent." Report to the Wisconsin Music Educators Conference, University of Wisconsin, Madison, Wisconsin, October, 1980.

Cooper, Irvin and Kuersteiner, Karl. **Teaching Junior High School Music.** Conway, Arkansas: Cambiata Press, 1973.

Dale, Philip S. **Language Development — Structure and Function.** Chicago: Holt, Rinehart and Winston, Inc., 1976.

Fowells, Robert M. "The Changing Voice: A Vocal Chameleon," **The Choral Journal** (September 1983): 11-16.

Gordon, Edwin E. **Learning Sequences in Music: Skill, Content and Patterns.** Revised Edition. Chicago: G.I.A. Publishers, Inc., 1989.

Gordon, Edwin E. **Advanced Measures of Music Audiation.** Chicago: G.I.A. Publishers, Inc., 1989.

Gordon, Edwin E. and Woods, David G. **Reference Handbook for Using Learning Sequence Activities.** Revised Edition. Chicago: G.I.A. Publishers, Inc., 1990.

Gordon, Edwin E. and Woods, David G. **Why Use Learning Sequence Activities?** Chicago: G.I.A. Publishers, Inc., 1985.

Harper, Robert. "General Techniques for Teaching Learning Sequence Activities." **Readings in Music Learning Theory.** Darrel L. Walters and Cynthia Crump Taggart, eds. Chicago: G.I.A. Publishers, Inc., 1989, 105-112.

Harper, Robert. "Specific Techniques for Teaching Learning Sequence Activities." **Readings in Music Learning Theory.** Darrel L. Walters and Cynthia Crump Taggart, eds. Chicago: G.I.A. Publishers, Inc., 1989, 113-128.

Hausmann, Charles S., March, Hunter C., Miller, Samuel D., and Roe, Betty G. **World of Choral Music.** Teacher Edition. Morristown, New Jersey: Silver Burdett & Ginn, Inc., 1988.

Herman, Sally. **Building A Pyramid of Musicianship.** San Diego, California: Curtis Music Press, 1988.

Jordan, James. "Music Learning Theory Applied to Choral Performance Groups." **Readings in Music Learning Theory.** Darrel L. Walters and Cynthia Crump Taggart, eds. Chicago: G.I.A. Publishers, Inc., 1989, 168-182.

McKenzie, Duncan. **Training the Boy's Changing Voice.** New Brunswick, New Jersey: Rutgers University Press, 1956.

Rutkowski, Joanne. "The Junior High School Male Changing Voice: Testing and Grouping Voices for Successful Singing Experiences." **The Choral Journal** (December 1981): 11-15.

Swanson, Frederick J. **Music Teaching in the Junior High and Middle School.** Englewood Cliffs, New Jersey: Prentice-Hall, Inc., 1973.

Swanson, Frederick J. "The Proper Care and Feeding of Changing Voices." **Music Educators Journal** 48 (1961): 63ff.

Swanson, Frederick J. "The Vanishing Basso Profundo Fry Tones." **The Choral Journal** (May 1977): 5-10.

Swanson, Frederick J. "Voice Mutation in the Adolescent Male: An Experiment in Guiding The Voice Development of Adolescent Boys in General Music Classes." Unpublished doctoral dissertation, University of Wisconsin, 1959.

Walters, Darrel L. **Learning Sequence Activities Introductory Manual.** Chicago: G.I.A. Publishers, Inc., 1987.

Wierson, Colette. "The Application of Music Learning Theory to the Teaching of Middle School General Music." **Readings in Music Learning Theory.** Darrel L. Walters and Cynthia Crump Taggart, eds. Chicago: G.I.A. Publishers, Inc., 1989, 154-167.

ABOUT THE AUTHORS

TERRY BARHAM, Associate Professor of Music and Director of Choral Activities at Emporia State University, Emporia, Kansas, earned degrees from the University of Illinois (M.S.) and the University of Oklahoma (B.Mus.Ed. and Ph.D.). A native of Oklahoma, he has taught at the University of Arizona, University of Wisconsin - La Crosse and Viterbo College. While teaching high school in suburban Chicago, he sang with the Chicago Symphony Chorus. He has served as guest choral conductor and clinician at the high school and junior high level in twelve states. His research on the choral music of Vincent Persichetti has been published by the ACDA **Choral Journal.** Dr. Barham has lectured widely on the changing voice in adolescent boys, including presentations at the 1991 Oklahoma Music Educators State Convention, the 1989 Kansas Music Educators State Convention, the 1986 ACDA Western Division Convention and the 1984 Arizona Music Educators State Convention. At the 1987 National ACDA Convention, he served on a panel which discussed the state of junior high choral music. In 1984, he was an Associate Conductor of the People-To-People National Student Chorale which toured China, Japan, and Hong Kong under the auspices of ACDA. In 1989, the Emporia State University A Cappella Choir, under Dr. Barham's direction, toured England, France, Belgium, and West Germany. At Emporia State University, he directs three choirs and teaches conducting and choral music education classes. He also serves as Editor of the Kansas ACDA Newsletter.

A native of Arizona, DAROLYNE NELSON earned degrees from Arizona State University (B.Mus., Choral Education, M.M., General Music). A teacher for thirteen years at McKemy Middle School, Tempe, Arizona, she also has served as Music Consultant for the Tempe (AZ) Elementary School District. Choral enrollment at McKemy Middle School has increased from 38 singers to 270 during her tenure. She has been nominated by her colleagues for the Arizona Teacher of the Year and the Arizona Music Educator of the Year awards. Ms. Nelson has conducted numerous elementary and junior high honor choirs in Arizona and, in 1990, the Arizona Elementary-Junior High School All-State Choir. At Arizona State University, she has presented workshops on middle school teaching strategies, musical theater, choral techniques and the boy's changing voice. Her choirs have achieved recognition for their superior musicianship through performances for local, state, and national organizations, district, state, and regional honor choirs and Arizona television specials. Fourteen of her students were selected to sing in the 1987 Western Division ACDA Junior High Honor Choir in Los Angeles. Ms. Nelson's leadership roles include serving as Vice-President of ChoDA (Choral Directors) for the Arizona Music Educators Association and Chair for the 1990 Arizona All-State High School Show Choir. Currently, she serves as Chair of the Arizona ACDA Repertoire and Standards Committee for Jazz and Show Choirs.